The Pig War

An I CAN READ History Book

by Betty Baker

Pictures by Robert Lopshire

Harper & Row, Publishers • New York, Evanston, and London

British
Land

The
Island

U. S.
Land

Twenty miles out

in the big sea bay

is a little island.

Many, many years ago,

in 1859,

no one knew

who the island

belonged to.

Farmers came

to live on the island.

They thought that it

belonged to America.

But on the island

was a small fort.

The men in the fort

traded with Indians.

The traders thought the island

belonged to the British.

6

Every day

when the sun came up,

the men in the fort

put up the British flag.

7

A farmer named Jed
said, "By dogs,
don't they know
who this island
belongs to now?"

"Maybe they don't,"

said his friend.

"The British have been here

a long time."

"That may be," said Jed.

"But we are here now."

The farmers made

a big flag.

And every day

when the sun came up,

up went the British flag

and up went

the American flag too.

"I say,"

said the British captain,

"who do they think

this island belongs to?"

"I never saw

such a big flag,"

said a trader.

"It may be big,"

said the captain,

"but they know nothing

about putting it up.

We will show them

a thing or two."

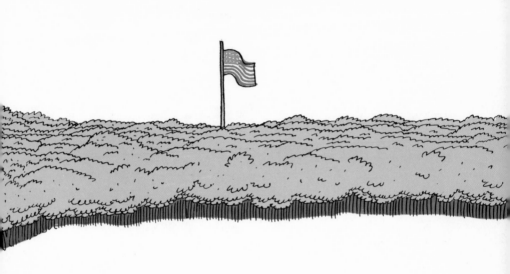

When the sun

came up again,

up went the American flag.

Up went the British flag.

And a drum in the fort

went BAR-RUMPITY-DUM,

BAR-RUMPITY-DUM,

BAR-RUMPITY-DUM-DEE-DUM.

15

"That's kind of nice,"

said a farmer.

"By dogs," said Jed.

"If they can do that,

so can we."

"No, we can't,"

said his friend.

"We do not have a drum."

"You have a fiddle," said Jed.

So when the flags

went up again,

BAR-RUMPITY-DUM

went the British drum.

18

And *scritty-scrit-scree*

went the fiddle.

It upset the chickens,

and they could not lay

any eggs.

"Down the British!" said Jed.

"Look what they

made us do

to our chickens!"

"I will stop

playing the fiddle,"

said his friend.

"No," said Jed.

"If they have a drum,

we must have a fiddle."

The British captain said,

"With that fiddle,

they cannot hear our drum.

What is better than a fiddle?"

"My bagpipes," said the trader.

When the sun came up again,

the flags went up.

The fiddle *screed*,

the drum BAR-RUMPED,

and the trader played

on his bagpipes.

The captain's pigs

did not like bagpipes.

They jumped out of the pen

and ran . . . and ran.

"Pigs in the gardens!"

called the farmers.

26

"By dogs," said Jed.

"Flags and fiddles

were just for show.

But this is war!"

Guns banged.

One pig went down.

The rest ran off.

The captain came

with men from the fort.

"You farmers shot my pig," he said.

"You must pay for it."

"No," said Jed.

"Look what the pigs

did to the gardens."

"This is what comes
from flags and fiddles,"
said the captain.
"You should go home
to America."

"This *is* America," said Jed.

"No, it is not,"

said the captain.

"It is British land.

And if you do not pay

for the pig you shot,

British soldiers will come

and take you away."

Jed's friend said,

"*That* for British soldiers."

And he threw a potato

at the captain.

Soon potatoes were flying

at all of the traders.

The captain called,

"I will be back

with soldiers and guns."

"This looks bad," said Jed.

The farmers sent for help.

Soon boats came

with American soldiers.

"They can't do that,"

said the captain.

He sent for help too.

Three British warships

came over the bay.

The men on the ships

looked at the farms.

The American soldiers

marched up and down

and looked at the ships.

For a long time

the island was still.

The flags went up,

but no drum BAR-RUMPED.

No fiddle *scrĕed*.

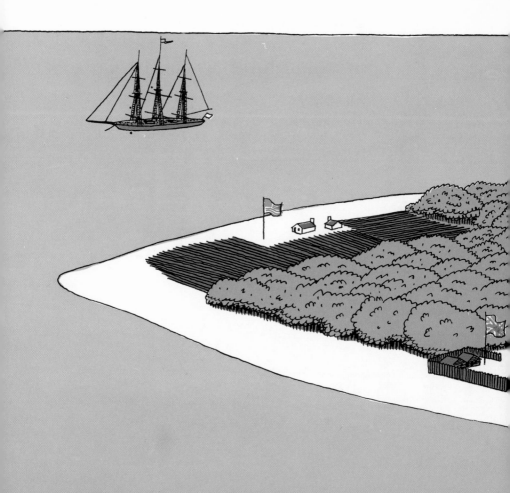

The men on the ships

looked at the farms.

The soldiers marched.

The farmers worked.

And everyone waited

for something to happen.

"Winter is coming,"

said the farmers.

"The soldiers are eating

all of our food."

"Yes," said Jed.

"And soon we will have

nothing for winter.

45

We must do something."

"What?" said the farmers.

"I want to think," said Jed.

He went for a walk

around the island.

"How do," said Jed. "What

are you doing way out here?"

The captain said,

"I am hiding the pigs.

The men on the ships

want to eat them all."

Jed laughed and said,

"I was just thinking

how much we miss that drum."

"The fiddle was nice too,"

said the captain.

"Nice flag you have," said Jed.

"You have a nice flag too,"

said the captain.

"A little big, but nice."

"It is not too big

for this island," said Jed.

"This island is so big

it could have two flags."

"Maybe it could," said the captain,

"if someone would pay for the pig."

"We do not have much," said Jed.

"But we will give you

potatoes and eggs all winter.

That will pay for the pig."

"Good," said the captain.

"And I will give you two pigs

to pay for the gardens."

The men shook hands.

"By dogs," said Jed,

"now all of us

will eat this winter."

The captain sent the ships away.

Jed and the farmers

said good-bye to the soldiers.

For twelve more years
no one knew
who the island
really belonged to.

But every day

when the sun came up,

up went the British flag.

And up went the American flag too.

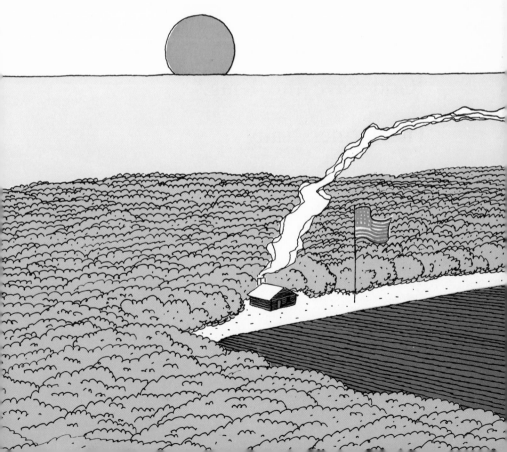

The drum and fiddle and bagpipes

became the island band.

Every Sunday

they played one song.

The British called it

"God Save the King."

The farmers sang

other words

and called it "America."

Today the island

belongs to America.

It is part

of the state

of Washington.

The fort is still there.

So are some of the gardens.

And they still tell about
the Pig War.
But they may not tell it
just this way.